Helping Your Young Child Cope with a Parent's

Jerilyn Marler

Author of *Lily Hates Goodbyes*
Quincy Companion Books

Helping Your Young Child Cope with a Parent's Deployment

by

Jerilyn Marler

Quincy Companion Books
http://quincycompanionbooks.com
http://jerilynmarler.com/publisher

Quincy Companion Books
PO Box 219221
Portland, OR 97225
http://quincycompanionbooks.com
http://jerilynmarler.com/publisher

*Helping Your Young Child Cope
with a Parent's Deployment*

Print format ISBN: 978-0-9852348-0-5

Electronic release: November 2011
Trade paperback printing: March 2012

Ordering Information
Special discounts are available on quantity purchases by
corporations, associations, and others. For details, contact
the publisher:

Jerilyn Marler, Publisher
Quincy Companion Books
PO Box 219221
Portland, OR 97225
jerilyn@jerilynmarler.com

Contents

Nobody Likes Goodbyes

Raise your hand if you like saying goodbye. Anybody? No? I didn't think so. Deployment is dreadfully hard for adults. *It's even worse for children.* I hope this handbook will provide guidance, encouragement, and ideas to help you help your young child to not just survive the separation, but *thrive despite the separation.* When it's easier for your child, it's easier for you, too.

In the next two chapters we'll talk about specific tools and activities that can help your child. But first, let's look at the bigger picture of what most children go through and what they need when a parent is away for about a billion days.

Note! The "Pulling It All Together" section includes all resources mentioned in this book (and some bonus resources you should know about!). The list is alphabetical with the Web address (URL) for each resource.

That resource list, with hyperlinks, is available online at **http://jerilynmarler.com/resources**

Goodbye = Stress

Saying goodbye is stressful. Missing a loved one is stressful. Not knowing when the parent will be home is stressful. Knowing that a parent has a dangerous job is stressful.

You see where I'm going with this. Children are ***stressed*** when a parent is on deployment.

As adults we can tell when we're stressed. If we're taking care of ourselves, we act wisely to do something about it: call a friend, do a vigorous workout, walk around the block, let the tears flow. We eat healthy food, get regular exercise and enough sleep. (You're doing all that, *right?* You've got to take care of yourself so that you can take care of your child.) Recognizing we're stressed takes a level of self-awareness that younger children simply don't have. It's up to us, the parents, to help them.

As of April 2011, the military community included 1.8 million American children under the age of 18. That's a lot of potential stress. And grief.

Reactions Children May Have to Deployment

The Department of Defense's **2011 Deployment Guide** provides amazing detail on all aspects of preparing for and getting through deployment for the military member, spouse, and children. The guide lists these types of reactions children may have to deployment at different stages of development.

Toddlers may
- worry about basic needs
- have temper tantrums
- exhibit sullenness
- have difficulty sleeping

Preschoolers may
- regress (e.g., start having trouble with potty training again)
- worry about basic needs

- become clingy
- be afraid to sleep alone
- act out and test limits more than usual
- be afraid that the service member will get hurt

School-age children may
- worry about the safety of the deployed parent
- complain often and loudly
- become aggressive
- place significance on missed family events (e.g., birthdays, church, sports, or play)
- act out and test limits more than usual
- miss the deployed parent most during routines or activities they normally did or enjoyed together (e.g., dinner, bedtime, school plays, recitals, sports events, etc.)
- have trouble sleeping
- have less energy than usual
- be irritable and overreact to seemingly minor things

Adolescents may
- worry about the safety of the deployed parent
- act out and test limits more than usual
- exhibit lower self-esteem
- exhibit misdirected anger
- have problems in school
- lose interest in hobbies and activities
- cry more often to release pain and anxiety
- refuse to have contact with the deployed parent
- have physical symptoms (e.g., loss of appetite, stomach aches, insomnia, headaches, nightmares, restlessness, nausea, etc.)

(Source: The Department of Defense's 2011 Deployment Guide)

You can see that children of any age can suffer terribly because of a parent's absence.

How *you* cope with and respond to the deployment will directly affect how your child copes and responds. Are you adjusting well? Maintaining social contacts? Keeping an overall positive outlook? Are you communicating to your child that you are confident you will all be fine through this experience? If so, your child will be more relaxed and happy. If you are uptight and angry, or gloomy all day, or withdrawn from family and friends, your child will respond with fear and anxiety. A child's behavior is very often triggered by, or is a direct reflection of, the parent's behavior.

If you or your child is struggling, get help! There's no shame in asking for assistance. It doesn't mean you're weak. It means you're smart to recognize that each of us has limits to what we can handle on our own, how much stress we can bear. The military provides extensive mental and physical support. Take full advantage of it. Spouses and children can receive free, anonymous, non-medical counseling sessions from Military and Family Life Counselors and from Military OneSource.

The Deployment Health and Family Readiness Library contains a wealth of information and resources to help. Reach out.

The Good, the Bad, and the Normal

Emotions are neither good nor bad. They simply are. Nobody—no matter what age—should be made to feel ashamed for any emotion. They're a part of our humanity. It's what we *do* with emotions that can get us into trouble.

I want to emphasize this: *help your child understand that all emotions are okay, even the "bad" ones.* Negative emotions are a normal response to a difficult situation.

Imagine that you're feeling an intense negative emotion. Maybe your mother just made (another!) critical comment about your parenting style. You are ready to blow a gasket. Your spouse says, "Stop feeling that!" What do you want to do to your spouse? Probably something that would put you in timeout for a month. But if your spouse says, "You're really angry. How can I help?" You feel understood. You feel heard. The intense emotion loses its grip. You can take a deep breath and think more calmly. Children need this kind of help from their parents to recognize the emotion, be reassured that the emotion is okay, and take healthy steps to deal with it.

Hello, Emotion. What's Your Name?

Children use play to express their emotions (which they often don't understand and have no words to describe) and to cope with stress.

Ask your child, "What are you feeling?" and you'll most likely get a shrug and the answer, "I dunno." So what's a parent to do?

Watch body language and encourage talk and/or play to express it.

When children are stressed, when they're in emotional *dis*tress, they tend to be restless (some parents say wired!), moody, and sometimes out of control. Watch for signs of anxiety, restlessness, quick anger, easy irritation. Those signs probably mean that your child is feeling something intensely. Use your judgment to determine the most likely emotion under the circumstances.

Use non-critical observing statements and then offer a suggestion that involves play in some form. The observing statement helps the child associate the name of the emotion with the feeling. The suggestion helps the child learn healthy ways to deal with the emotion. It's also important to explain that grownups feel the same things, too.

"You seem to be restless. Let's go outside and run around for a bit to work off some stress."

"You seem to be bored. Maybe it will help to do something different. Let's go make some bubbles in the bathtub."

"You seem to be sad. Are you thinking about daddy? I feel sad sometimes, too. Let's sit together on the couch and read a book. Which one would you like?"

"You miss mommy very much. Your mommy misses you very much, and she is working hard at her job so that she can come home. It's okay to miss your mommy while she's at work. I miss her, too. Let's draw a picture for her and send it to her right away."

"You seem to be lonely. I feel that way sometimes when I think about daddy. And then I think about you and it makes me happy. Let's play with your puppets. Show me what makes you happy."

Acknowledging all emotions is not the same as accepting all behavior that results from the emotions. If your child behaves in dangerous or inappropriate ways, you must address that immediately. **But do your absolute best to remember that this is your child *hurting. Aching. Sad.***

Respond with as much patience and love as you can muster. After you've handled the immediate issue, talk about the emotions that led to the misbehavior. Suggest other ways for your child to respond differently in the future.

A Crying Shame...?

Support (and even encourage) your child to cry. Humans respond to sadness, frustration, and joy with tears. It's a universal—and unique—human characteristic. We cry because of traumatic experiences, loneliness, stress, heartbreaking loss, pain, and frustration. We also cry in response to joy, happiness, and relief. Crying is natural and normal for everyone at any age. (I mean adults, too!) It's also *necessary.*

When your child cries, respond with supportive, non-judgmental statements. For example: "You're very sad. Crying will help. Cry as long as you need to. I'm right here." Offer comfort and a steady, calm presence. Some children cry briefly. Some cry for a long time. It takes whatever time it takes. Crying can't be rushed and it shouldn't be cut off because you become impatient.

Your child will process intense emotions by crying, releasing toxins through the tears. The act of crying and the release of toxins are therapeutic. After a bout of crying through which you have comforted and supported your child, the child's mood will be brighter. Your child will feel better. Give a big hug, say how glad you are that the child was able to express the emotion, and suggest something fun to do to help ease the transition from sadness to lightness.

Not the Child's Fault

Young children can mistakenly feel responsible for a parent going away. They might feel that the parent's absence is punishment. They might experience the absence as abandonment—thinking that the parent chose to leave. These are huge, weighty concerns that will rock any child's self esteem and sense of security. If one parent chose to leave, will the other one, too?

You can help by talking about the deployed parent being *at work*. Explain that daddy's job means he has to work in another country for awhile and that as soon as his work is done, he'll be back. Talk about the jobs other members of the family or close friends have, so the child sees that jobs are a normal part of the adult world. Reinforce the message that daddy wants to be home and is away because the job requires it. If possible, arrange play dates with other military children who have a parent on deployment so that the children can draw strength and reassurance from each others' experiences. *Other kids are getting through it. I can, too.*

Alert the Media! (Well, at Least Teachers and Caregivers)

Make sure that the other adults and caregivers in the child's life know what the child is going through. Share the timetable. Keep teachers and daycare providers aware of problems you're seeing. Ask them to watch for signs of distress that you might not see. Working together, you can all be part of an active, loving, supportive network with the goal of helping your child thrive.

What Else Do Children Need?

Consistency. Children are particularly vulnerable during deployment because there's so much uncertainty. They always need consistency and a steady daily routine, but they need it most during deployment. They might bounce around like a pinball, but they need to know that the walls they bounce against are rock solid. I'm talking about emotional bouncing, figurative walls. Children test limits. It's their job. It's how they learn the boundaries of their world. It's your job to give your child a safe, consistent place to do that exploration.

Communication. Children also need honest (but age appropriate) communication. Your child will have lots of questions. Answer whatever you can. Be respectful of your child's curiosity. When you don't know an answer, say so. If you can find out the answer, do so. Questions open the door for more discussion about emotions and how to deal with them. Take advantage of those teaching moments.

Use caution, however. Don't talk about your own fears and worries in detail. Don't transfer your concerns to your child. Reassure your child often of *both* parents' love. Reassure your child that the deployment will end and that you'll be together again. Talk about how joyful that will be. Talk about how you'll get through it *together.*

Time and attention. This might be hard to give. Your spouse is away. You're dealing with your own emotional upheavals and functioning as a single parent under extraordinarily difficult circumstances. You have more demands on your time, less energy to respond to those demands, and you're tired. I get that.

But does your child get that? No, of course not.

What is your priority? Your child. Honor that priority.

If your schedule is too full to spend focused time with your child, fix it! (The schedule, not the child.) Cook simpler meals. Shop closer to home. Cut back on your social network time. Involve your child in more of your own activities, such as cooking.

When you're talking/interacting with your child, do it with your whole mind and heart. Let everything else drop away. Concentrate on this moment. Those beautiful eyes. That sweet heart that is a part of your heart. Act as though there is nothing more important in the world than your child.

Because there isn't.

Now obviously you can't do this all the time. But when you have the opportunity, do it. Don't let yourself off the hook with excuses. Your child *needs* your attention. Give it. If you're watching TV while you play a game with your child, you're cheating the child. If you're working on email or Facebook or your blog while your child is talking about the school day, you're cheating your child. These are golden opportunities to connect. Embrace them. Give your child **at least** 30 minutes of your full, undivided attention every day. Every. Single. Day.

Lots and lots of love. Can you hear it too often from your spouse that you're loved? I doubt it. Children need to hear it often, too. Say it in many ways and under different circumstances. Don't save "I love you" for just bedtime. Love your child throughout the day. Start every morning with a cheerful, happy greeting. Use hugs, kisses, high fives, pinky promises, and holding hands to show your affection.

As I was writing this book, I asked my granddaughter Lily, now five years old, what she thinks are the most important things that at-home parents can do for their children during deployment. She thought for a moment and then said, "Hug them. Kiss them. Say I love you." She's been through it. She knows.

Love and attention are the sunshine and soil that will help your child grow a healthy sense of self and belonging. Be generous with both.

In the next two chapters I'll describes 22 ways you can help your child build and sustain a connection with the away parent. Some of the ideas come from my own experience with Lily when her daddy (Scott, my son) was at sea. I've also collected suggestions from readers of my children's book *Lily Hates Goodbyes* and through research. We all benefit by sharing what we've learned. If you have additional ideas, please let me know. My email address is on the copyrights page of this book. I'll incorporate ideas into a future revision of this book.

Preparing for the Goodbye

This chapter lists 10 activities you can do before deployment that will help your child (and you!). Many of these can be implemented after departure, of course, but there's huge value in planning ahead.

1. Stuffed animal adventure

The soon-to-be-away parent and the child choose a stuffed animal (or other item that holds meaning for both) that the parent will take on deployment. Agree on a name for the animal. Before departing, take some photos of the stuffed animal with the parent and child together. During deployment, the away parent photographs the stuffed animal in interesting or amusing locations around the world. When possible, the away parent shares photos by uploading them to Flickr or Facebook or by emailing them to the child (and spouse!).

~Tip! Scott and Lily chose identical stuffed hippos. Lily named hers Rex. Scott named his Lily the Hippo. When Lily saw Scott's photos, she could hug Rex and feel closer to her daddy. Scott took photos of Lily the Hippo all over his ship and in fun places around the world while on shore leave.

2. Memory object

Give the child a pendant or locket with a photo of the away parent and child together. This is a natural idea for girls, but it can also be helpful for boys. It can hang beside the bed, or be carried in a pocket, or used as a zipper pull. The point is to give the child a personal, visual touchstone that is easy to access. If you have more than one child, try to make the object unique to each one.

~Tip! I had photo pendants made for my granddaughter, daughter-in-law, son, and for me. Although my son is now home from deployment, I still wear the pendant daily and get more compliments on it than for any other jewelry I've owned. People respond with warmth and interest when they see the photo.

3. Videos

Take videos of the deploying parent with the child and of the whole family together. Capture goofy moments, tender moments, and full belly-laugh moments. Your child will watch them over and over.

~Tip! Children love to hear stories about when mommy and daddy were little. One day I told Lily a story about when her daddy was her age (4 years old). Scott thought the words to "Teddy Bear's Picnic" were "Watch them, catch them, *underwears!*"(instead of unawares). Lily laughed long and hard with sheer delight. She asked me to tell her again. She laughed again, and asked me to repeat the story. I grabbed my iPhone and recorded her while I told (and retold) the story four more times. Lily is now 5. The underwears video is still one of her favorites.

4. Audio recordings and greeting cards

Think in advance about the holidays and milestones (such as birthdays) that the deploying parent will miss. Record messages now that the at-home parent can play for the child at pivotal moments during the separation. Your child will love hearing your voice and receiving the special cards with hand-written messages. Some planning now and a bit of time to get organized and prepared will pay huge dividends in boosted spirits for your child.

~Tip! Buy greeting cards that let you record your own message, in your own voice. Every time your child opens the card, it will be to hear *you.*

5. Flat Daddy/Mommy posters

Flat Daddy/Mommy posters are life-sized printed posters (waist up) of the deployed parent. Consider one for each occupied bedroom in your home so that everyone can say goodnight to the away parent and feel watched over by him or her.

6. Daddy/Mommy dolls

Holding a physical representation of the away parent is powerful. Children can carry the doll everywhere so that a daddy/mommy hug is immediately available. Here are three fine organizations that provide mommy dolls/daddy dolls to military children.

The **Operation: Military Kids** program, which is called Operation Give a Hug, provides a doll with a clear plastic holder to insert a photo of the away parent's face.

US Deployment Dolls are customized with the loved one's face, matching combat duty outfit, custom name tags, and a 20 second heart recorder.

The **Daddy Dolls** organization creates large and small dolls with the deployed parent's full-body likeness.

7. Photo mugs

Whether it's a plastic cup for kids or a ceramic cup for the at-home parent, photo mugs can warm your hands and hearts while you drink hot chocolate or coffee or tea.

8. Un-celebrations

Birthdays are especially important to children. If a parent will miss a child's birthday (or the parent will be gone on his/her birthday), consider holding an "un-birthday" celebration before departure, complete with cake and ice cream and candles. Take lots of photos and make lots of copies so that the deploying parent and the child have some. On the actual date, your child will know that the away parent is remembering the happy celebration with the child from across the miles.

~Tip! The un-celebration idea works for any important milestone.

9. United Through Reading Military Program

The **United Through Reading Military Program** helps children and deployed parents connect through the experience of reading together. United Through Reading provides books at deployment sites around the world. Also, with a little advance planning, the deploying parent can choose books before departure to take along. Before Scott deployed, he, Amanda (his wife), and Lily chose six children's books for him to take along. During deployment, using the equipment and processes provided by United Through Reading onboard, he made video recordings of himself reading the books to Lily. She received the recordings on DVDs. You can enhance your child's experience by having copies of the books at home so the child can read along with the parent. It's heart-healing for a child to watch mommy or daddy on the computer screen or TV (through the DVD player).

~Tip! Scott took a photo of Lily the Hippo sitting atop the video camera that recorded Scott reading the books. It was another visual reminder for Lily of how her daddy was keeping her close to his heart while away.

~Tip! Record a favorite bedtime story so that the away parent can be part of the nightly tuck-in routine.

10. Create a connection routine

Agree to a personal connection routine or "secret code" that specifically connects the child and the away parent. For example, the departing parent can promise to blow a kiss to the sky every night when the first star appears.

~Tip! Lily believed that her daddy could hear anything she said to the moon. She'd see the moon and talk to Scott and then say good night, blowing a kiss to the sky.

Lily waiting for daddy's ship on
homecoming day
March 2011

During Deployment

This chapter describes 12 more activities you and your child can do together to help the deployment time pass pleasantly and to strengthen the connection across the miles.

11. Memories for Daddy/Mommy box

Children like to save special objects, drawings, postcards, and other meaningful items to share with the away parent when the deployment is over. Let the child decide on the container and then decorate it. Keep it handy and don't censor what the child chooses to put in it.

~Tip! Lily decorated a sturdy box and glued photos of her daddy to the outside. She saved drawings and colorings, special objects, cards she received from relatives, and anything else she wanted to show her daddy. Within five minutes of arriving at the house on the day he got home, Scott and Lily were sitting side-by-side on the floor going through the box contents with delight.

12. World map and calendar

Get a map large enough to see the names of key cities around the world. Make sure you can stick pins in it or that tape will hold to the surface. Hang it on a wall at your child's eye level. Using age-appropriate stickers, mark where you live. Include stickers for the locations of other people who are important in your child's life (grandparents, for example) to help give a sense of scale and inclusion. Talk about where in the world the away parent will probably be. Always be mindful of OPSEC (operational security), even with your children. "We think Mommy will be mostly in this part of the world." When you can share specifics about where the away parent is, add a sticker to the map.

Use stickers on a calendar to identify key dates and to help the countdown to visits or the big end-of-deployment reunion. Let your child draw an X through the previous day. As the Xs grow, the child gets a concrete view of time passing. Each X gets you one day closer to the happy hello at the end of deployment.

~Tip! Make "stickers" using photocopies of the away parent's face with a big smile. Use those stickers for each identified (or approximated) location on a map and on special dates on the calendar.

13. Family fun night

Children need routine to feel safe and secure. It's important to include fun time in that routine. One possibility is to set up one night a week for games. Include extended family members, if possible. Keep the mood light. Play board games or charades or (weather permitting) hide-and-seek outside. Let the child participate in deciding on the evening's activities and let the child direct the activity to the extent that is safe. Celebrate creativity. Be open to spontaneity.

~Tip! Lily and I go on adventure walks. We head outside with no specific destination or activity in mind and let the adventure unfold. Sometimes we discover bugs or interesting rocks. Sometimes she runs and runs, burning off stress. Sometimes we just walk and talk. It's precious time together.

14. Puppet time

Keep some puppets handy and encourage free form play with them. Your child will be able to express questions or emotions through a puppet that can't be said directly. Listen carefully. Be supportive. Ask questions. Provide reassurance.

15. Type email and Skype messages

While Scott was deployed and I was writing him an email, I asked Lily if she wanted to write a message to her daddy. She hopped onto my lap. She tapped long strings of characters and then she'd say, "What does it say? What does it say?" I tried to pronounce the unpronounceable strings, which cracked us up. Then she told me what the strings meant. I added her translation, carefully typing exactly what she told me. She always wanted me to read it back to her. Here's an actual transcript written the day after Halloween:

Gjjbbjhyjubnrbn

Hi Daddy! I love you so much. I want to see you.

Ukguhhikgihuuh

I liked the new Lily Hippo pictures. My favorite was the girl with the Lily Hippo.

Ikuyihkjkuhugkgyjgghjitmjliku8kukyukhkhknoo;gigilg;ilo

And I have sparkly fingernails. I love them so much. I had fun with Olivia trick or treating. And then I danced in a contest. Olivia let me hold her lantern. And she shaked her shark fin. But I wanted to win. I got fifty thousand candy. My favorite is chocolate. We ran out of candy at the door because there was so many kids. And we needed to say "there's no more candy!" when people was here.

Lkjjk,j,k,n,okjk;ljjhlhhohjojlmlm/mkljhjlhjklhkhlhhhlhkh khlklllIbkghooyoypotpti;9yooy9kkkkkknnllglkl"g;flglllh llglll;gokkkkgkghkkggkjggjgjgjgjfjkjdodjgjhjgj

Hi (again), Daddy. I love you so much. I want to see you. Again. And again. And again. Goodbye Daddy! I love you so so much!

———————

Can you imagine how much this message meant to her daddy? Priceless.

One day we were wildly fortunate to send a Lily-typed message to Scott while he was actually at the computer on his ship. He responded almost immediately. We wrote back and forth (gibberish and all) several times before he had to report for duty. The live interaction was particularly exciting for Lily.

16. Explore your neighborhood, town, state

With a little research you can identify an amazing list of nearby activities, museums, parks, and cultural centers, many of them with no or low cost, or with military family discounts. Once a week or once a month or whatever cadence works for you, set out together to explore some place new.

~Tip! Create a list of the new places you've explored together. Let your child rate the experience (perhaps using stars). The child will have fun talking about those experiences with the returned parent, and the highest star count activities will make wonderful family time outings together.

17. Learn a new skill

Rock climbing, anyone? Or bowling? Or drawing/painting? How about playing the piano? Work together to learn something new. Take photos and videos of your development to send to the deployed parent. Mark your progress. Set a goal to achieve a certain level of accomplishment by the time deployment ends. Make it fun!

18. Keep a journal

Encourage your child to write or draw in a journal every day. There's no right or wrong thing to include—whatever the child is thinking about or wants to share with the away parent is fine. This is a great opportunity to help your child talk about and find healthy ways to deal with intense emotions of grief and loss. Visit **Deployment Journal for Kids** for more information about getting the most value out of journaling.

19. Create photo books

Use a digital photo service such as snapfish.com or shutterfly.com to create a photo book of images captured since deployment. Let the child participate in choosing the photos and designing the book. Have the book shipped directly to the away parent. If you can afford it, order two (or more) and share them with grandparents and keep one for yourself. Look through the album with your child and talk about what the away parent will think and feel and say when looking at the same photos.

20. Send care packages

Involve your child in thinking of things to send to the away parent. Help the child pick out funny greeting cards or postcards and write or draw a personal message. Let your child choose at least some of the candy bars or protein bars or other goodies you include. Send recent photos. Put lipstick on you and your child and make kiss marks on a card. Giggle together as you pack the box, anticipating how the away parent will be delighted with everything inside. Your child will benefit from contributing to the away parent's happiness.

~Tip! When we learned that Fridays were funny tee-shirt days aboard ship, we visited Goodwill and found several that we knew would make Scott smile.

21. Together at the table

Keep a framed photo of the away parent on the dinner table so that you're all together while you eat or work on art projects or do homework. Talk about the away parent often. Play guessing games about what the away parent is doing at that moment, or having for dinner, or thinking about. Help your child talk about the away parent as a vivid part of daily life.

22. Countdown to reunion

As the deployment end date gets closer, make the countdown a fun part of your daily routine. Cross off a date on the calendar. Chant a meaningful phrase (such as "only 10 more days!" or "Mommy's coming home!") three times and then give each other a huge hug. Keep the celebration low key initially. Recognize that as the day gets closer, your child's tension level will rise. Boost the amount of time you spend in play together, and redouble your efforts to help the child express emotions safely.

Plan the homecoming together and involve your child as much as possible. Make special decorations. Decide on the menu for the first meal together and make sure it's something that the child can help prepare. Make up a poem together and write it out or sing it to the melody of a favorite song. Recall together some of the highlights in your lives during deployment and write them down. That'll help the child have fresh memories of happy times to share.

Make sure that your child feels involved in planning for and executing your homecoming activities.

Putting It All Together

Let's face it. Deployment separations can be brutal. Remember that you can choose how to respond to the challenges. Also remember that your choices will have a direct impact on how your child gets through the separation. Help your child through the turbulent emotions by remaining calm and steadfast in your reassurances that everything will be okay.

This book suggests 22 tools and activities for you and your child to make the time more fun. Choose the ones that fit your life and budget. Make up your own activities. Join a parent support group for social interaction for both you and your child. The point is to be interactive and engaged with your child as much as possible. It will be healing for both of you.

You can do this.

And guess what? You don't have to do it alone! Here are the resources mentioned in the book (and some bonus resources you should know about!) pulled together in a handy alphabetized list. This list just scratches the surface of the many wonderful organizations committed to helping you and your child through the agony of deployment separation. Some Internet searching focused on your city or state will help you find local resources.

This list, with hyperlinks, is available on my website at http://jerilynmarler.com/resources.

Resource List

Daddy Dolls Organization
http://www.daddydolls.com
Large and small dolls of the parent's full-body likeness.
They also sell plastic and ceramic photo mugs and other
mementos.

The Department of Defense's 2011 Deployment Guide (PDF)
http://www.militaryhomefront.dod.mil/12038/Project%20 Documents/MilitaryHOMEFRONT/Service%20Providers/ Deployment/2011_DeploymentGuide.pdf
Extensive resource that covers everything from describing
deployment to planning for it, to getting through it. I
recommend that every family facing deployment go through
this document carefully.

Deployment Health and Family Readiness Library
http://deploymenthealthlibrary.fhp.osd.mil/
Provides fact sheets, guides, and other information
products on topics such as family readiness and resources
for service members and families, educators, and clinicians.
Another great site to bookmark.

Flat Daddies and Flat Mommies
http://www.flatdaddies.com
Provides life-sized printed posters of the deployed parent
that can be a steady, welcome presence in a child's room.

Journals for Military Kids
http://www.deploymentkids.com/journals.html
Describes how to help your child get the most value from
the journaling experience.

Lily Hates Goodbyes, by Jerilyn Marler
Available on Amazon, Barnes & Noble, Powell's Books, and
other online retailers for only $6.95
Lily Hates Goodbyes is a storybook especially for young
military children to help them survive and thrive during a
parent's deployment. Learn more in the *About Lily Hates
Goodbyes* section at the end of this book.

Military Child Education Coalition
http://www.militarychild.org
Extensive resource with trainings and programs for parents,
students, educators, and healthcare professionals who
work with military children.

Military One Source
http://www.militaryonesource.mil
An outstanding one-stop shop for resources to help with all
aspects of military life, including deployment, family and
recreation, health and relationships, career and education,
financial and legal, crisis and disasters, and community.
Bookmark this site!

Operation Give a Hug
http://www.ogah.org
Provides mommy dolls and daddy dolls with a clear sleeve
to hold the away parent's face.

Operation Homefront
http://www.operationhomefront.net
Provides emergency financial and other assistance to the
families of service members and wounded warriors.

Operation: Military Kids
http://www.operationmilitarykids.org
Offers a broad and deep array of programs and activities
for children affected by deployment. They also offer a
daddy doll.

United Through Reading Military Program
http://www.unitedthroughreading.org/military-program/
Helps children and away parents stay connected through a
shared reading experience. Parents read books aloud,
videotaping the reading. Children receive a DVD of the
recording and can watch on their television and read along.
It's a remarkably powerful experience for everyone in the
family.

US Deployment Dolls
http://www.usdeploymentdolls.com
Cuddle-sized dolls customized with the loved one's face,
matching combat duty outfit, custom name tags, and a 20
second heart recorder.

About the Author

Jerilyn Marler with granddaughter Lily, 2010

I'm a writer/editor with over 30 years of experience with technical and non-fiction work. In 2010 I wrote *Lily Hates Goodbyes* for my 4-year-old granddaughter because she was distraught by her daddy's deployment aboard the USS MOMSEN. It helped her so much that I published it in early 2011 for all children who hate to say goodbye. In August 2011 I established Quincy Companion Books, an imprint of Wyatt-MacKenzie Publishing, and released *Lily Hates Goodbyes* through international online book sellers such as Amazon, Barnes & Noble, and Powell's Books.

From sixth grade through my junior year of high school I attended Kodaikanal International School, a boarding school in the mountains of southern India. Memories of my long, painful separations from my parents helped me relate to Lily's experience 46 years later.

My father was a Navy doctor during my first six years. My first husband was in the Army when we married. My son is a Navy officer. I've lived the military life as a child, a spouse, and a parent. My passion is helping military children thrive despite the challenges they face.

I currently live in Beaverton, just a few miles from Portland, Oregon, with Dan, my husband (who is a former Navy man), and our two tabby cats.

Jerilyn Marler website:
http://jerilynmarler.com

Lily Hates Goodbyes book page:
http://lilyhatesgoodbyes.com

Lily Hates Goodbyes Facebook page:
https://www.facebook.com/LilyHatesGoodbyes

About *Lily Hates Goodbyes*

Two versions available as of March 2012:
   updated Navy version
   new All Military version

Lily *really* hates goodbyes. Her daddy is deployed for about a billion days and she's swamped with scary emotions. She feels angry, sad, stubborn, and naughty. Her mommy helps Lily understand her emotions and cope with them in healthy ways. Lily blows kisses to the sky to wish daddy goodnight and she saves drawings and mementos in the Memories for Daddy box. Lily finds ways to be happy despite the separating miles. She adds stickers to a calendar to help count down the days to daddy's return. When the big day finally, finally arrives, she jumps joyfully into her daddy's arms. *Lily loves hellos!*

Lily and her ever-present bunny Quincy are reassuring, comforting, and inspiring companions. One mom shared that her daughter carries the book with her everywhere because she never knows when she's going to feel sad about daddy being gone. Another parent told me that her three kids talk about having "Lily moments," which helps them keep perspective and remember how to handle their turbulent feelings. *Lily Hates Goodbyes* is the perfect book for all young children who hate goodbyes.

http://lilyhatesgoodbyes.com

For ages 2-7
32 pages, full-color storybook
Published by Quincy Companion Books
Vibrant illustrations; perfect bound
Retail only **$6.95**
Purchase online through Amazon, Barnes & Noble, Powell's Books, and other major online book retailers

Sample Praise for *Lily Hates Goodbyes*

"For a number of years I have worked with military families and tried to help them in time of need. One such time is deployment—anxiety and worry levels increase and adjustment becomes difficult, especially for the children. I have found one book specifically written for such occasions which helps to allay the anxiety and provides cognitive techniques for the child to use as he or she worries about the deployed parent. *Lily Hates Goodbyes,* by Jerilyn Marler, is such a book; it is well written and illustrated, and can be read by the child (2nd grade or higher) or by a parent to the child. I highly recommend it."
—B.G. Quesenbery Jr., Ph.D.
Licensed Psychologist, Charleston, SC

"I see hundreds of children's books a year, since I not only do reviews, I work in the industry. *Lily Hates Goodbyes* is as good as they get, on par with the best. I'd love to see a hard bound, Smythe stitched version, that could better stand the test of time, and childhood use, so that it could be handed down for generations to come, it's that good, that it should be a family heirloom for any military family."
—David Broughton, Children's Book Editor & Reviewer

"My husband is a cop and there are times when he goes away for trainings. I read this book to my kids (ages 8, 5, 3) and they immediately connected to little Lily."
—Book Loving Mommy Blog Review

"I highly recommend this book for any caregiver, parent, or family therapist working with a child as he/she adjusts to a change in their family environment. As a family therapist, I love that Jerilyn also has a page at the back of the book with a list of ideas/activities to help create a discussion with families about ways to help each other cope with a parent away for a period of time. ... It is a must read for any child whose parent(s)/caregivers are serving in our military and away from home!"
—Books in the Burbs Blog Review

"I was very impressed with the natural and simple way Jerilyn Marler tells this story. She could have spoken down to children or over their heads, but instead she is right on the mark with this one. You will love it. Best of all, you will appreciate it so much."
—Biblio Reads Blog Review

"Marler uses the last page of *Lily Hates Goodbyes* to offer suggestions on how parents can help their children benefit from the book, including the deployed parent reading it with

the child before departure. No, *Lily Hates Goodbyes* will not make the pain of separation any less, but it may make it easier for a child to cope with and discuss it. And that can lead to happy endings."
—Technorati: Bob on Books Review

"*Lily Hates Goodbyes* is a remarkably simple, yet beautiful book in both message and illustration. Children are drawn to the book and enjoy reading about a little girl who, like them, sometimes feels sad and sometimes feels angry and sometimes blows kisses to the moon. The military's Family Readiness Groups should stock up on copies of *Lily Hates Goodbyes* as it is a must-have for any child facing a parent's deployment."
—The Book Trotter Blog Review

"This book is really well written and beautifully illustrated with colorful drawings in a really accessible style. The goal of the book—to help young children deal with the long absences and unknowns of having a parent in the military—is clear, but unlike other books that are written with such a specific purpose, it doesn't sacrifice anything to reach that goal. The writing is perfect, the verse easy to read and poignant. There are a few repeated refrains such as 'a billion days' and 'Lily hates goodbyes' that lend a sense of poetry to the prose."
—The Family That Reads Together Blog Review